for Fred Swann

TOCCATA BRILLIANTE

Sw. Full organ *ff*, 4' coupler and Mixtures (no reeds)
Gt. Full organ *fff*, mixtures, reeds, 4' coupler
Ped. Full pedal 16',8',4' Sw. to Ped. 8'

TWILA PARIS
Arranged by FRED BOCK

Triumphantly, with energy

BGK1057

Gt.
ff
Sw.
Gt.
legato
Sw.

Broaden
Gt.
solidly
a tempo

allargando
a tempo
sforzando on
ffff
white pedal
glissando

Dr. Fred Bock
1939 - 1998

FRED BOCK was one of the most recognized and respected leaders in the church music world. He was a noted composer, arranger, clinician, studio musician, organist, pianist, choral director, and music publisher. With over 600 compositions and arrangements in print, his works continue to sell to choirs and keyboard players. His anthems have been sung by leading choral groups around the world and remain strong sellers many years after their initial releases.

Fred served as Editor of the *Hymns for the Family of God* hymnal, the best-selling, non-denominational hymnal ever published. He was the President of Fred Bock Music Company and was widely regarded as a leader in the music publishing field, serving on various committees and boards for ASCAP, the Church Music Publishers Association, and the National Music Publishers Association.

Fred was a keyboard-recording artist for both the secular and religious markets. He delighted in being the conductor of the Candlelight Christmas Concerts in Disneyland, which involved two 1,000-voice choirs, a 50-piece orchestra, bell choir and soloist, and thousands in the audiences. His work as a studio musician can be heard on dozens of films and television shows, numerous recordings, and one very Haunted Mansion in Disneyland, USA.

"We build too many walls and not enough bridges."

- *Sir Isaac Newton*

worship BRIDGES

Music should be a unifying force that allows the Body of Christ to speak as One voice to the Almighty. Too often music has been used to create walls and isolate one group from another within the same congregation. **Worship Bridges** endeavors to unify our church families by creating a series of resources for church musicians that merge the greatest songs and melodies of today with the traditional forms and styles that have endured for centuries. The goal is nothing less than to enable music to once again be a source of unity for the Church, not a tool for divisiveness or separation. The world needs a vibrant and unified Church now more than ever. This series enables us to rejoice in the rich legacy of our past while celebrating the creativity of today.

"Music can change the world because it can change people." - *Bono*

00148454 BGK1057 $9.99

8 88680 07795 2

www.FredBock.com

Fred Bock Music Company

EXCLUSIVELY DISTRIBUTED BY HAL•LEONARD® CORPORATION

ISBN-13: 978-1-934596-77-7

50999

9 781934 596777